PINK LADY

PITT POETRY SERIES

TERRANCE HAYES
NANCY KRYGOWSKI
JEFFREY MCDANIEL
EDITORS

PINK LADY

DENISE DUHAMEL

UNIVERSITY OF PITTSBURGH PRESS

Published by the University of Pittsburgh Press, Pittsburgh, Pa., 15260
Copyright © 2025, Denise Duhamel
All rights reserved
Manufactured in the United States of America
Printed on acid-free paper
10 9 8 7 6 5 4 3 2 1

ISBN 13: 978-0-8229-6736-1
ISBN 10: 0-8229-6736-7

Cover art: Photograph of the author's mother, provided by the author.
Cover design: Melissa Dias-Mandoly

for the next generation:

Ben, Nick, Max, Zach, Brody, and Alex

CONTENTS

Prodigal Prayer

I kneel before my mother, trying to get her slipper socks
over her swollen feet. Then she presses the remote control
on her recliner to push her to an almost standing position.
Once upright she is not steady enough to get to the walker alone.
Our goal—to get her to the bathroom on time. Shame. Then tears.
She soaks her Depends because of a water pill
that's supposed to help her puffy legs.
But nothing, it seems, is helping.

This is a week before her second fall, the bad one.
Before the pneumonia and sippy cups. Before her right arm
no longer works. Before the fingers on her right hand go numb.
Even when I put a pen between them, she will not be able to sign
her name. This is before the hospital and more sippy cups,
one with the Nemo logo on loan from her great-grandson.
This is before her stint in rehab where Doug will try to teach her
to put on socks with a blue plastic device she slips over her calf,
a rope she holds in her good left hand. She will keep cheese popcorn
in the seat of her walker and offer some to Doug who looks
like Matt Damon. She will be like a girl with a crush. She misses
my dad—dead eleven years—but some days is angry he left her.

This is before I drive her twenty-year-old Toyota to see her
in the Catholic nursing home where the priest reminds us
"this too shall pass." I will think about my mother passing
water, about her ultimate passing, her eventual death.
I question if her pain will indeed pass, if what is passing
through her body will keep on passing, looping into her,
the morphine drip not enough to dilute the pangs in her spine,
her neck, sciatic nerves running down both of her legs.
A chorus of nuns will sing while playing maracas
and tambourines. One sister will drop her percussion
as she falls asleep mid-song. It will be funny, then touching,
then ultimately so profound I become my mother
taking care of a two-year-old me.

I become my mother who puts a pillow under my stomach
when I can't breathe. With cupped hands she pats my back
just the way the doctor shows her, the doctor who says
to pretend my back is a bongo drum. When the fever comes,
she rubs my arms with alcohol and flips the pillow
under my head to the cool side, puts a bucket near my bed
as I am sure to vomit. When we go to La Salette Shrine
to see the Christmas lights, I mistake the basin for donations
near baby Jesus's cradle as a puke pail. All the kneeling people
around us laugh, guessing perhaps what a sick child I am
and how many nights my mother sits up with me with Vicks
and antibiotics, inhalers and picture books to help calm the cats
who live in my chest making strange wheezing sounds.

I'm allergic to cats and dogs and even stuffed animals, grass
in the summer and leaves in the fall, lilacs which blossom
in spring, and my lungs can't take the winter cold. No wonder
my mother wraps the statue of the Virgin Mary she kept
by her marital bed and puts it in the bottom drawer.
The Virgin helped her get pregnant,
but after me, she's had enough.

Soon my mother is again with child anyway. She tells me
how I still wanted all the attention and as soon as my mother
started nursing my sister, I'd put my hand in the diaper pail
and stare at her, daring her to make me stop. When JFK was shot
and my mother wept in front of the television, I blocked her view
with my two year old body and peed on the carpet.

Now it is my mother peeing, mortified, drenching
her nightgown. She once changed my diapers and now
I change hers. Oh little mother, my helpless daughter,
please forgive me for I have sinned. It has been years
since my last confession, my last therapy session.
Hail Maryjane brownies, please help my mother's appetite,
please help her to sleep. Hail Mary, full of grace,
please heal my mother's bruised face.

Last Picnic

We bundled her up and took her to Iggy's in Narragansett.
It was still chilly, early May, as she perched in her hooded jacket
on the seat of her walker so she didn't have to slide onto the wooden bench.
Her great-grandsons ran to the playground spinner and slides.
My mother's chowder flipped in the wind and landed on her lap.
I wiped her up with a bunch of napkins.
My sister rescued the rolling bag of clam cakes.

Summer of Love

Decades before my mom went
to live at Mount St. Rita Health Centre,
she worked as a nurse there
taking care of elderly patients—
mostly nuns back then. She was surprised
when they swore, their guards
down at last. They no longer
wore habits, their gray hair
popping up in clumps or braided
down their backs.
                        Around that same time
Sinead O'Connor was sent
to a Catholic reform school in Ireland
where the Magdalene Laundry girls,
grown old by then, were abandoned
in an adjoining building—no
medicine for their pain.
As punishment, Sinead was made
to sleep in the same room, their cries
making her feel scared and useless,
no way to help.
                        Centuries before,
St. Rita, the Patron Saint of Impossible
Causes, was married at twelve, abused.
Later in life, she became a nun
at Saint Mary Magdalene Monastery after she levitated
into the Italian convent. As an infant,
bees swarmed into her mouth
but didn't sting. I was allergic to bees
and no saint. St. Rita made peace, mended
political feuds.
                        My mother could mend
feuds within the family but wasn't always
overtly political. I once asked her about
the Vietnam War and the Summer of Love.

She said it was all a blur—*I was busy*
those days working and taking care of you.

What My Mother Left Behind, What She Discarded

she'd given away the frying pans too heavy for her to lift
the wrapping paper rolls (too much for her arthritic hands
to mess with scissors and tape) all her shoes with heels
the TENS machine that never really helped
my dad's bicentennial quarters (he collected one from every state)
the bag of flour (too heavy) the lawnmower and chainsaw
(Tony took care of the lawn by then)
the toolbox except for one screwdriver (because you never know)
the lanyards with ID cards from Foxwoods and Twin River casinos
her Better Homes and Gardens cookbook set
the Encyclopedia Britannica
the 1965 dictionary with the marbled endpapers
the potting soil and tomato trellis and expired makeup
the record player and all her Johnny Mathis albums (CDs were easier)
the sewing machine the knitting needles

she was down to just a few bowls and cups

she had already emptied her house of all the grade school cards
my sister and I made for her
the pipe cleaner hearts our misspelled love

Butterfly Poem

She has an Orange-tip necklace,
Holly Blue spoon rest, Monarch clock,
a throw rug crocheted with Swallowtails.
Each birthday and Christmas,
she'd say, *Get me anything—*
as long as it has butterflies on it.
Did she want a short colorful life
rather than the long drudgery
of motherhood? Did she want to slide off
her nurse's uniform and sprout
Painted Lady wings? Now that she's in
the nursing home, she is divesting herself
of her Essex Skipper slippers,
her Speckled Wood vase. *No more presents,*
she says. *No more clutter.* I tell her
about Dolly Parton's butterfly tattoos. My mother
is in too much pain for another needle, even one
filled with pretty ink. She's in too much pain
to fly to Florida ever again. But, if she could,
she'd make one more trip to Butterfly World.

Purple Poem

Her forehead is purple, black
eyes circled with what looks like football
players' grease, except her cheeks
are unevenly flushed, bruises streaking
down past the rim of her glasses. She is grateful
she wasn't wearing them when she fell. Her elbow
is plum, her upper arm eggplant. Her violet feet
are so violently swollen she can't wear her slippers.
Her robe is lavender fleece with a zip-up front
which seems like a bad design for my mother
now that she can't bend to reach the zipper's bottom
to mesh the teeth. When my dad was still alive,
they both went to see *Purple Rain* at my suggestion.
I was surprised they listened to me and more surprised
they both liked it. Now Prince is dead, and my father
is dead and my mother asks me to bring
her lilac summer pants to the nursing home
even though it's Christmas. The buttons
on her jeans frustrate her. Her cotton pants
have a drawstring. And, besides, the nursing home
is so warm. I stick a piece of cardboard
under the window sash so she can get a little air.
My brother-in-law unscrews the round-the-clock nightlight
and puts in another piece of cardboard
so my mother can sleep. She can't
wear her eye mask because she can't
lift her arms. At mass, the priest's cassock
is purple satin—purple, that unrhymable
color, that word you can't use as an end word
in a sonnet, that color of grapes and wine, of wild
pansies and wisteria, that color that mixes
blood and sky, fury and despair. The priest
comes with the host to each wheelchair
as the nuns sing "Joy to the World." By spring

my mother's bruises will fade to green,
matching the veins that thaw
and cascade in her hands.

Wackadoodle

My mother was a fan of the word,
often peppering her sentences with it.
She visited me in Florida the day after
Trump won in 2016. When I'd sent her a ticket,
I thought we'd both be celebrating
the first woman president. When I picked her up
at the Fort Lauderdale airport, nothing
looked different. I was baffled, sure
that the planes of the world would stop flying,
their wings too heavy with grief.
I know, of course, planes don't have feelings—
and I was projecting onto those silver beasts.
My mother and I tried to talk about
other things, but we kept coming back
to America's withering future. Once in a while
my mother would say, *We just have to*
give him a chance, I guess. And I would nod
though deep inside I knew Trump was a flimflam
sham, that things would get worse.
We didn't know yet that that this would be
my mother's last visit. We didn't know
she would wind up in a nursing home ravaged
by COVID-19. We didn't know the U.S. would be ravaged
by an insurrection. She was ravishing
that November and men kept trying to talk to her,
no hint of death anywhere in her torso.
One old dude wearing a Scarlet's Strip Club cap
cornered her while I was in a restaurant
bathroom. *All flirting is ruined*, my mother said.
All I can think of is that wackadoodle
grabbing women by the you-know-what.

My Mother in a Grass Skirt

in a hula dance pose
under the clothesline absent of clothespins or clothes,
her long hair strategically draped over her chest.

She is ten—it's 1946—
World War II has just ended, her older brother back home,
her older brother a father figure

who will walk her down the aisle when she grows up.
He bought her this gift,
this rustling skirt

which scratches her waist,
this artifact from the Pacific
where he was stationed,

where he saw a pregnant woman shot,
the only atrocity he'd ever talk about.
He was shellshocked, the word for it then,

and he woke up screaming
in the bedroom next to my mother's
and my Grammy would go in to soothe him.

He was six feet tall and 120 pounds,
not at all the way my mother remembered him
before he left, when he loved food

and made a snack of a butter and brown sugar sandwich
before my Grammy even finished the supper dishes.
By the time my mother married, by the time I was born,

he regained his weight and became an accountant—
through the GI Bill. For the rest of his life
he liked numbers and things he could control.

My sister and I loved him, our favorite uncle.
My mother hated this topless picture of herself.
Sometimes her brother's nightmares

disturbed her sleep and she'd doze off the next day in class.
She said the grass skirt made her look fat—
of course I know now it was much more than that.

Laundry Poem

My mother
could walk down
the stairs if she walked
backwards, hanging on to the
banister with both hands. She did her
laundry in the basement though we offered to
move the washing machine to her garage. *No, it's my*
exercise, she said, her second walker at the foot of the stairs
to meet her. She'd already tossed the dirty clothes down the stairs
in a bag, though sometimes the bag never made it down the whole way.
She used the seat of her walker to carry detergent and fabric softener. When the

laundry was done, she'd call my sister or me and ask us to bring up the basket
to her bedroom. It was hard to watch her slow painful climb back to the
first floor, her wrists flat on each step as she hauled herself up, her
primary walker waiting by the doorjamb. In dreams you climb
down stairs to visit your subconscious and climb back up
looking for enlightenment. My mother was doing
neither. Just trying to stay as long as she
could in her own home. *Please don't*
look at me, my mother said, so I
turned away, bracing
for her fall.

The Last Time I Saw My Mother before the Pandemic

was on Valentine's Day 2020. The residents who were able to sit up
gathered in the dining room. Pink Lady volunteers decorated it
with red tablecloths and streamers for a festive lunch. At first
my mother didn't want to go, but I talked her into it.
I brought my own food—supermarket sushi—and the residents
at the table were mesmerized by it. One had never seen raw fish before.
Another said her son eats it too, but she found it scary.
They had me read the ingredients aloud. Women from the kitchen
served small meals as Frank Sinatra crooned from a Boom Box.
I cut my mother's chicken for her. She was still getting used to eating
with her left hand. The server insisted I join in for dessert—
a slab of vanilla ice cream cut into the shape of a heart
with a drizzle of raspberry sauce, a silhouette of a lipstick kiss.

Barn Babies

Trying to keep its residents safe, the nursing home
suspends all activities. No sing-along Tuesdays, no Lifetime
movies with popcorn and juice. No physical therapy
for my mother. No strolls down the hall where she'd
keep a book on the seat of her walker in case she needed
a rest. No rolling into the family room with the curio cabinet
full of teacups, with the window overlooking the geese.
No bingo, no trivia night, no piano bar. And no Barn Babies,
my mother's favorite pastime. She and the other residents
were wheeled into the elevator, then down to the basement
where they could hold bunnies, kittens, and puppies,
where they could pet a diapered goat or lamb, a potbellied pig,
where they could watch the chicks and ducklings peck at food
pellets on the cement floor.
                      In trying to keep the world safe,
the rest of us shelter-in-place. In our absence, animals
take to the streets. As I walk nearly empty Florida paths
the chameleons and lizards are out in full force.
In Dania Beach, the next town north, Brian Wood
is making masks from the skins of Burmese pythons,
an invasive species taking over the Everglades.
                          Mountain goats
roam a seaside town in Wales. Wild deer look into an empty
Samsung store in Sri Lanka. Cows sunbathe on a Corsica beach.
Hundreds of monkeys surround the presidential palace
in New Delhi. A herd of goats runs through San Jose
stopping to eat plants from suburban lawns. Wild boar
and red foxes saunter through Israel, while fox cubs
frolic in a Toronto parking lot. In Bolivia, horses and llamas
trek a deserted highway.
                   And speaking of llamas,
their nanobodies could potentially be used as a treatment
for people infected with COVID-19. When I phone my mother,
a retired nurse, I tell her of this development.

Llamas! she says. *Let me tell the CNA. If llamas are that good for us, maybe we can get the Barn Babies back.*

Snow Globe

My mother tells me the nurses dress like astronauts.
Mount St. Rita's must go on the assumption
that any of the patients could be infected. The RNs complain
that it's hot under their masks and visors, gowns and jumpsuits.
My mother suggests the nurses open the window for air,
even though it's chilly, even though it's a nor'easter.
All they had to do was get me a blanket. Poor things,
they're working so hard. Then her room is a globe,
everyone's world shaken, snowflakes and stars.

Strength Training

I'd started a strength training class ($25 a pop)
after my mom's hands no longer worked, after her arms
hung weak by her sides and she didn't have the power
to pull up her pants. For two years I'd thought
about the class but was too cheap to register
when I could go to free yoga-on-the-beach
which met at the same time. Now, because of COVID,
the class can no longer meet. Now, because of COVID,
the beach is closed—not only to yoga, but also to walking
and sunbathing and swimming. Not so long ago
I stretched bands across my chest and held balls
between my knees while lowering my legs
onto a mat next to other women my age,
some of whom had been in car accidents
or had hip replacements, and others who, like me,
had never thought much about their muscles.
We'd talk about where to get the best Greek salad—
Giorgio's, now closed—or the hazards of driving
at night. So few cars on the road now. My mom dozes
on and off in the nursing home, using all
of her strength, her training to stay positive—
no more visitors, no more card games, no more matinees—
as she fiddles with her flip phone,
her numb fingers trying to call me.

Votive Poem

I take out the votive candles, bought before phones had flashlights, thinking they'd be a backup in case of a hurricane. Backup upon backup was always my way to prepare.

I light a red one and put my mother's picture near it—a makeshift altar. After her accident, I said novenas. My heart would wake me in the middle of the night like a crying baby—*thump thump thump.*

The sulfur puff brings me back to St. Joseph's, where I'd put a quarter in a metal box and light a candle for my father after he'd passed. My mother's in a nursing home, unable to attend Mass in her wheelchair. No more communion. No more Sisters of Mercy with their tambourines. No more visiting priests, only the memory of church or church on TV.

I light the candle each morning, snuff it out each night, careful the fire doesn't catch my sleeve.

Adaptation

Since she still can't receive any packages, my mother is running low
on dark chocolate and cheese popcorn. The staff hand out Hoodsie Cups
that come with wooden spoons like those I remember
from the grade school cafeteria. My mother doesn't have
the hand strength to deal with the splintery spoon or poke through
the frozen treat, so she lets the ice cream melt then drinks it.

Communique: Emails from Mount St. Rita's

Wednesday, April 8, 2020

It is with a heavy heart that I tell you that the predictions of the governor and health officials regarding the spread of Corona at our nursing home have come to fruition. Three more residents have tested positive. Their families have been contacted. We are not accepting any more packages but you can certainly send cards.

Wednesday, April 15, 2020

On Monday the nursing staff tirelessly swabbed all the patients on the 3rd floor and others on the 2nd. To date there have been 8 more positive tests.

Wednesday, April 22, 2020

The latest numbers of the virus are: 47 positive cases, 5 in the hospital, 5 expired, with 16 staff testing positive. We are talking to many of you regularly to give an update of our sickest residents.

Friday, April 24, 2020

To date, we have 51 residents who have tested positive for the virus, 7 expired, 17 staff testing positive.

Monday, April 27, 2020

As of this morning we have 58 positive cases, 7 deaths, 18 staff positive. Many residents are showing mild symptoms, but others are seriously sick. We are in close contact with those whose family members are very ill.

Wednesday, April 29, 2020

We now have 59 positive cases, 8 residents who have passed and 4 residents in the hospital, 20 staff members positive. Please understand that it is extremely difficult keeping up with the volume of calls. We are doing our best to update families.

Friday, May 1, 2020

We are still at 59 positive cases, but now with 11 deaths and 22 staff positive.

Tuesday, May 5, 2020

One more resident's test came back positive making our total 60 cases, 14 expired, 25 staff testing positive. We have been communicating with the Department of Health and we will begin retesting residents who were positive but whose symptoms have seemingly resolved.

Friday, May 8, 2020

Right now we have 62 positive residents, 17 expired residents, 25 positive employees.

Monday, May 11, 2020

Nine residents who were positive were re-swabbed and have come back negative. All families were notified with the results of the negative swabs. We, the staff, certainly needed that boost!

Wednesday, May 13, 2020

To date, we have had 67 positive cases, 18 deaths, 25 staff positive.

Wednesday, May 18, 2020

Residents have to get 2 negative swabs in order to be considered cleared from the virus. There is usually 7 days in between each swab. If your loved one gets 2 clean swabs we will be in touch with the good news.

Wednesday, May 20, 2020

We received the results for 19 negative "second swabs" today. This makes a total of 30 residents who've beat this virus.

Tuesday, May 26, 2020

We got the go ahead from the DPH to accept packages and flowers for the residents. They have to stay in reception for 24 hours before being delivered to your loved one's room. A belated Mother's Day bouquet would sure brighten the days of some of the residents.

Tuesday, June 2, 2020

I have been asked many times when visitors can start coming to the facility. This is something that we do not know just yet.

Flip

She has pretty much given up
calling Michele or me as it's too painful
to punch the buttons on her cell.
We call her at specific times, and usually
she is able to answer. *They stuck another swab*
up my nose. I'll let you know how it goes.
Yesterday she kept asking me to speak up,
and I could barely hear her. She grew
frustrated then started to laugh.
She was holding her flip phone upside down.

Monkey Mind (or, Could He Win Again?)

November 5, 2020

I know the worth of each state's electoral votes by heart. My neck pain
has stopped but has traveled to my elbow and wrist. "Three consecutive
deep breaths" written on post-its—one beside the coffee pot and another
on my bathroom mirror. How many times this fall have I been told
"remember to breathe"? When I was little I watched "Zoom"
(*Who are you? What do you do? . . . Come on and zoom zoom zoom a zoom*
went the theme song.) The kids featured on Boston's WGBH
were local celebrities and my monkey mind wonders what happened
to them.
   I recently started the Netflix series "Ratched," the origin story
of Nurse Mildred Ratched (before *One Flew Over the Cuckoo's Nest*). On her job
interview, she says she's not worried about patients throwing their own feces,
that nothing throws her. As a young nurse, my mother worked
in a psychiatric ward and a patient clobbered her on the back of her head
with a book. I only made it through the first episode of "Ratched." I wanted to
like it because I like Sarah Paulson. I'm glad she is getting work,
but I found the show trying too hard, too stylized, like "Mad Men"
but without as strong a narrative. Then I tried "The Queen's Gambit"
but I know almost nothing about chess which the boys I grew up with
called "chest" to see if we girls would blush.
            Even now, whenever I read
the word "titular," (used in every review, for example, of "Ratched"
referring to the "titular character") I feel self-conscious
because the word contains "tit." I remember a writers' conference
many years ago, and a famous poet wanting us all to go to a "titty bar"
(her words). I said something like, "I just checked in with my feminist principles
and the answer is no." But now strippers are seen as empowered
by some in the third wave and I guess I'll need a more nuanced answer
if she ever asks again. Not that "titty bars" are even open
during COVID. That famous poet couldn't have been third wave
all those years ago, could she? She's a few years older than I am.
Maybe she was more revolutionary, better read. I can't believe two grandpas
ran for President, the final election results still days away.
               You know
who I (early) voted for since no poet could be a Trump supporter,

could she? Remember in 2016 when there was a fake story that Trump
was going to invite an American poet of Scottish ancestry (who also played
the bag pipes) to his inauguration? I fell for it, for a few minutes, but I don't fall
for much anymore. I believe Trump's imaginary inaugural poet was known
for his limericks. When I was a kid I loved Lime Rickeys and Del's Lemonade,
a slushy concoction that lost fans because occasionally they'd slurp a seed
or piece of rind up through the straw. That only made me love Del's more—
its authenticity, its real lemons.

                      I bought a lemon once but it was red, a Kia.
For two years I kept returning to the dealer because the interior smelled like gas
and the workers would reattach some hose that kept coming loose.
One time, a mechanic said, *This car could catch fire at any minute,*
so I looked up the lemon laws but I had stuck it out with the Kia
too long for the laws to apply. I fought with the dealer, called
the Better Business Bureau.

                      Shortly thereafter, a therapist asked
Do you want to be right or do you want to be happy? All these years later I am
in group therapy on Zoom and the facilitator finally last week
let us talk about politics as she said it was the elephant in the room.
What if he wipes out social security in three years? What about the climate?
Two of us in the Zoom group had already been hit
by hurricanes this fall—a man in Texas and me. After each rain,
Campbell's Florida street is flooded so much that ducks congregate
and think it's a lake. Only an October snow stopped the fires from spreading
to Maureen's house in Colorado. And what about the overrun hospitals?
It's too late to contract trace now, writes *The New York Times*—
the virus is everywhere.

                      And what about my mother at Mount St. Rita's?
No visitors, no activities, thirty-two of her neighbors now dead. She survived
the spring and summer, but will she survive autumn? When will I
be able to see her again? My mother has type O blood, I keep telling myself,
and though its low rates of infection are anecdotal, I'll take it. I've forgotten
my own blood type—I think it's A or B, as I'm quite sure I was never
a universal donor. And I never had to worry about an Rh factor
since I didn't have kids. I remember pricking my own finger in junior high

and then testing for my blood type along with all the other students.
I bet kids can no longer perform this test because of COVID-19,
because of AIDS. For so many years my friends and I were afraid
to get HIV just the way we are afraid of COVID now. Condoms then.
Masks now. No dinner parties, no parties at all.

                                    I teach Zoom classes
and miss driving to and from school in my reliable Honda, the car
I bought after I junked the Kia. Some situations can't be saved.
I hope democracy can, even our half-assed version. I hope the seas
can be saved. Scientists just found a reef as tall as the Empire State building.
I remember how my mom had a panic attack when she took us there.
I was five that trip to New York and, though it wasn't the worst part
of my childhood, I wonder what it did to me, to see my mom come undone
in front of strangers. I love heights and rarely get dizzy, even on the scariest
amusement park rides or parasailing. As I welcome the rush, I wonder if I
am compensating for something. I wonder if I am getting compensated fairly.
When I was hired, I should have asked for more money, but I accepted
an offer immediately. The chair of the English Department seemed shocked
and then said, "Okay. I'll send over the paperwork."

                                           I didn't think
I was entitled. Not like our entitled candidates. Though Trump won
the 2016 election without the popular vote, he acted like Mr. Popularity—
cutting regulations, nominating nutjob judges, lining his own pockets
like the world owed him. I would have been a tentative president.
I would have worked with the other side, trying to get my enemies
to like me. Even now I leap from branch to branch by my monkey tail,
quite certain I'll never be able to calm my monkey mind until all the votes
are in. I surrender my brain, my body, my own white flag.

Now That My Mother Isn't Allowed to Walk in the Halls

the pain from her arthritis is getting even worse. She has been confined
to her room for over a year. The palliative care doctor is trying
another new med, but it gives my mom nightmares. Last night
she started screaming for Joan, her roommate, who pressed the help button
as my mother couldn't find her own help button, didn't know in that moment
she even had a help button. Yesterday my mom told me they'd stopped
feeding her. When I call the nurse's desk, Maria tells me she was confused
but still ate half her pancakes. My mom asks me why I won't come to visit.
For a minute she's forgotten about COVID and the extra snacks in her drawer.
In another nightmare, she is part of a medical experiment. She laughs a little
now that she realizes it was all a hallucination. Maybe she's watched
too much horror on Netflix, she says. *And you won't believe this,*
but in another dream there was a man in my bed! And it wasn't
your father. I say, *Have fun, but be careful—I don't want another little sister.*
And I am so relieved when she laughs, that she gets my joke,
that I tell her another. Michelle Wolf says that the virus is nature's way
of saying to the world, *Go to your room and think about what you've done.*
Soon my mother will be in another room, the ICU.

ER

Deb, the ICU nurse, who once worked with my mom,
tells my sister and me she was a great mentor.
When my mom's back was too twisted to lift
patients anymore, she became an ER secretary
processing insurance and other irksome paperwork,
prioritizing who'd see the doctor next.
Deb said my mom liked the power, having been
bossed around by docs so many years,
and my mom smiles under her tubes and nods *yes*.
My mom mostly worked third shift
and often told us great, sometimes gruesome,
stories at breakfast. A man with a lightbulb
jammed in his butt. A lady-of-the-night's overdose.
The drunk who tripped on a curb
and needed 100 stitches to close up his scalp.
Your mom was always ready to help, Deb says.
She taught me a lot. Two decades before *ER*
premiered, my mom said her job
would make a great TV show. ER *was okay
and you can't fault George Clooney. But we
lived the real thing*, Deb says. *Didn't we, Jan?*

New Rules

In the ICU, we can visit her two at a time.
On June 18th, my sister brushed my mother's teeth
and held a pink basin to her chin to spit.
On June 30th, my mother told me her bangs
scraped her forehead. I took bobby pins
from my hair to pin hers back.
On July 2nd, my mom puckered up
so I slipped off my mask
and kissed her right on the lips.

Beginning

One of the first days my mom's in the ICU, I try to describe
The Blacklist's latest episode, "Nachalo." Characters
come back from the dead to explain to Elizabeth Keen
her secretive past, how Reddington and her birth mother
Katrina were simply trying to protect her. *Nachalo*—
I look it up—is Russian for "beginning." My mom had slept
through her favorite show, the hospital TV unable to record it.
The episode is full of black and white liminal space soliloquies
and the more I try to elucidate the plot, the more my mom
drifts away, also somewhere between the colorful now
and her monochrome past. She recognizes my sister and me,
then asks for her car keys to go home, though her Toyota is junked
and her house sold. She came to the ICU in an ambulance
via the nursing home where she needs no keys except maybe
the metaphorical keys to understanding life and death. She doesn't
see my father or any bright light yet. When she says
I thought I'd be leaving today I ask her if she means "leaving
the planet" and she says no. She thought she'd go
to a regular hospital floor. She can't see the machines
glowing around her and has grown used to the tubes,
not understanding how sick she really is. *Liz's birth mother
had Liz's memory erased after a fire on Christmas*, my sister says.
The season finale is next week. My mother looks at us and blinks.
On her wrist—a yellow DNR bracelet and a pink one
that reads FALL RISK. Congestive heart failure, staph infection,
fibrosis of the lungs. *Please don't let these doctors do that to me.
Yes, I'm miserable, but I enjoy most of my memories.*

What My Mother Said in the ICU

I hope all these animals don't bother your asthma.
I want to go see your dad now.
Who are you?
I can't take any more.
I feel lousy. There, I've said it.
Would you mind if I go? Will you be OK without me?
Ouch. Ouch. Ouch.
It's fine.
Will you stay with me once I decide it's over?
My mother stopped by, but now she's gone.
Sometimes her mouth kept moving
though she made no sound.

Generosity

She asked me to buy neck pillows
for anyone at Mount St. Rita's who admired hers—
nurses going on plane trips, a physical therapist
with a pinched nerve. She'd find out
the employee's favorite color
and I'd send them to her from Amazon.

In the ICU, a CNA bragged about her teenage son
getting his driver's license and my mother told her
to take $5 from her purse to give him,
even though my mom had no purse with her.
When I visited, she told me to get her wallet
and take myself to a nice dinner.

Just months before, during the worst
of COVID, as I was Zooming with her,
she lifted her afternoon snack to the screen,
a paper plate with three crackers
and a slice of American cheese—*I can't eat*
all this. Come on, have a nibble with me.

While She Can Still Speak

I record my mom singing "A Bushel And A Peck"
and send it to my nieces to play for their boys
who are all under 12, all too young
to visit the ICU. My mom has a bandage
on her nose from where the ventilator cut her,
and clear tubes of oxygen in her nostrils. Blue
veins squiggle her forehead as though her youngest
great-grandson has scribbled there. The boys
barely notice and send back their own videos—
Ben, Nick, and Max say, "We love you!"
then their mother pans over to the dog,
"And Ringo does too!" Zach, Brody, and Alex
sing "You Are My Sunshine." My mom
always hated our cell phones, the way they
distracted us away from her. But now she wants
me to hold my screen so she can see, so she can hear
the boys' song over and over again, her head
gently bopping back and forth on her pillow.

Independence Day (Hospice)

July 4, 2021

She says, *Who am I?*
She says, *Pray for me.*
She sounds like the country.

News

When I visited her I'd ask how she was
and at first she'd try to be cheerful—
A little better or *Not so bad.*
But soon she started answering
Lousy or *How do you think?*
It was then the hospice nurse
told me this question
was not recommended—
too much stress for my mother
to answer in a jovial way.
I have always hated this question
myself, the reflex, the expectation
the one being asked will say, *Great!*

At the wake, I forgave every person
who asked how I was doing.
How could they have known?
The hospice nurse said it's best to just listen.
Or bring news of the outside world.

That's Where You'll Find Me

My mother's hospice roommate is playing
Israel Kamakawiwo'ole's version of "Over the Rainbow"
which bleeds into "What a Wonderful World." My mom
is sleeping or drugged or a combination of both. I step
into the hall, afraid my sniffling will wake her.
When I come back to her bedside, I hold her hand, say
Hail Marys as she mouths along. Then she shouts
My top left drawer! I hold up her TracFone, a picture of dad,
a plastic rosary. *No no no*, she says and I fail her
once again. Israel Kamakawiwo'ole died of respiratory failure,
like my mother will soon, her troubles melting
like the Brach's lemon drops atop her bureau.

Another Summer of Love (2021)

My mother stopped wearing a bra
in Mount St. Rita's Hospice
because the straps hurt
her shoulders. I called her a hippie
and put a flower in her hair.

Ready

Her eyes open once
but they are cloudy and look through me.
A volunteer Sister who comes by to give
my mother communion decides
it's too dangerous. My mother could choke.
The Sister says a prayer over her instead
and offers me my mother's host. Though
I haven't been to confession in decades,
I say *yes*. I am ready to believe.
The Sister says, *God is ready for your mom.*
Your mom is getting ready for God.
My eyes drift to my mom's curled hands.
My mom drifts somewhere in her own God-clouds.

Ensure

A white foam coats my mom's lips, pills
she hasn't swallowed yet. The nurse tells me
to try to get her to drink an Ensure. When I ask
my mother, she shakes her head. When I ask
What about a little water? a scary voice comes from
deep inside, a hoarse yell, *I said no!* This takes me
back to my childhood, getting scolded,
and for the rest of the visit I stay quiet.
I take my mother's hand only after
she drifts off. I warn my sister before she goes up
for her turn. Because of COVID restrictions
at hospice, my sister and I can only go
to my mom's room, one person
at a time, after we are swabbed,
for "compassionate end-of-life" visits.

As I wait for Michele in the lobby, Father Robert
asks if I'm okay. I'm slumped, staring
at my phone, not even playing
Words with Friends to pass time. I tell him
my mother is not doing well.
He asks if she's had the Last Rites.
I tell him she'd want them. He says
Let's do it tomorrow—10 a.m. Later my sister
and the hospice nurse say Mom
seems better, a little more responsive.
I worry that she'll yell at me again tomorrow—
How dare you bring a priest! I worry
she'll have swallowed what she's been asked to,
ensuring us she can handle more suffering.

Sacrament

The hospice receptionist lets my sister and me
go up with Father Robert, who performs
the Sacrament of the Anointing of the Sick.
As he prays over my mother, she seems to wake a bit.
He dabs oil on her forehead and into her palms.
He breaks off a tiny piece of the host which seems to dissolve
in her mouth. I give her a splash of orange juice
from her sippy cup. Then Cindy, the nurse my mother never liked,
squirts more morphine under her tongue. After the priest leaves,
my sister and I stay, against COVID protocols. At one point
my mom comes to and says, *Make sure dad knows the priest came.*
The Sister who prayed over my mother a few days ago says,
"She's getting close." And I think of the Supremes' song
"You Can't Hurry Love." You can't hurry death.
No, you just have to wait. My niece's vacation
starts in five days, her family's first getaway
since the pandemic. I am sure my mom will work around
that date, as she's always loved Kate. But I am wrong—
my mom will die as my niece and her husband and kids
are on their way to Vermont. They will turn the car around.
My mom will die the day before her 85th birthday. I knew
there'd be no cake or candles, but I thought maybe I'd sing to her
and she'd move her mouth a little bit.

Sweet Day

I notice my mom's feet hang over the side of the bed,
an impossible move for her to make on her own.
She can no longer stand or even hold herself up to sit.
A CNA tells me my mother always got out on that side
of the bed when she still used her walker, when later
she slid into her wheelchair. The CNA shrugs—she's seen
stranger things. Mom is docile today—quick to smile
and sleepy. She lets me give her cranberry juice
from her sippy cup. She lets me hold her hand again.
A nurse tells my sister to get enough sleep and remember
to eat. Cheryl, the receptionist in the lobby, says to me
I know you are exhausted, but one day
you'll remember these days as the sweet days.

The Universe

Elsa hit Massachusetts today. I feared the hurricane
would swipe my condo in Florida, but it skirted Hollywood,
instead pummeled the west coast of the state, then formed again.
Remember when talk about the weather made for idle chitchat?
Now weather is a matter of life and death—tropical storms,
tornados, wildfires, drought. Rain floods the streets
so that we can't leave for hospice until 2 p.m.
Mom mostly sleeps. When I tell her *I love you*
she opens her eyes and says *What?* She asks me if I need
the bathroom so I ask her if she needs the bathroom
even though there is no way to get her there, even if
she could stand or sit up. She doesn't
wear Depends anymore, just a big pad under her
and a Foley to take care of her urine. Each day she shrinks
a little more. Today she refuses anything to drink.
Her lips are purple-black and thin. The bobby pins
I clipped into her hair are long gone, her bangs slicking back
on their own. When she opens her eyes again, they roll up,
as though she is looking at something beyond me.
I want to think my mom is nearer to seeing
and understanding the universe, the future of the planet.
But my sister says my mom looked beyond her too
and at one point said, *Dear, I have no idea.*

Mercy

Just yesterday her great-grandsons
picked up baby toads and let them hop
from their thumbs. I hold her hand
and rub her arms and tell her
she can let go. The toads landed
in the grass where the boys
were afraid to step on them.
I'm thinking about my mom
landing somewhere soft and green
when even my rubbing
hurts her, when she says,
Please don't touch me.

Teaspoons

When I arrive the nurse has just given my mom Ativan
because she was agitated, her breathing labored. I can't
rouse her with kisses on her forehead or by telling her I'm here.
My cousin Johnny sent her a birthday card which I read aloud.
My mom's chest is lifting up and down, a stubborn machine,
her breathing a wheeze. It's not called the death rattle
anymore, it's not called the Last Rites, it's not even called
pulling the plug. The different lexicon doesn't ease my worry.
The CNA says my mom had two teaspoons of water
and juice for breakfast. Teaspoons? Because I am a poet,
I think of Prufrock's declaration—
"I have measured out my life with coffee spoons."
Because I love pop culture, I think of the Crash Test Dummies'
song. I find myself humming "I've watched the summer evenings
pass by/I've heard the rattle in my bronchi." How easy it is
for the young to think of death in the abstract, how easy it once was
for me, but now I am here staring at Death, watching it settle
into my mother. "Someday I'll have a disappearing hairline/
Someday I'll wear pajamas in the daytime." I'm humming
and crying. To distract myself, I look up how long a person can last
in hospice without eating. To distract myself, I hum.

Nourish

My mother's nipple
from where I once fed
pokes through her hospice gown
as though it is one of the snaps.
I'm not sure I should touch
her breast, rearrange her,
as so much of her body hurts
and she's at last floating
on morphine. Her nipple
once nourished me
but now nothing can nourish her
as she refuses all food.
I'm feeling useless, wanting
to preserve my mother's
dignity, when a nurse
with a solution so obvious,
so simple, pulls up the bedsheet.

Baby Mouse

July 11, 2021

My mom died this morning at 9:55.
I'd gotten up early as I'd heard
clanking. My sister found a baby
mouse in her sink and droppings
on her stove. She scrubbed
as my brother-in-law trapped
the mouse in a jar and let it go.
I ate oatmeal, walked, and took
my shower. I was getting dressed
to visit my mom at Mount St. Rita's
when the phone rang. I could hear
my sister talking in her office
and assumed she was speaking
to one of her daughters. When I went
downstairs to tell her I was ready
to leave, my sister put her hand
over the receiver and mouthed,
Mom died. I ran upstairs to call
Kerri who was also going to visit
and caught her in the parking lot.
Wait for us, I told her. Michele
and I didn't want her to go in alone.
The twenty-minute drive seemed
like an hour. What did the mouse
mean, if anything? Why weren't
we more prepared? We'd had
over a month to get ready for this day.
Kerri stood near her car. The three
of us masked up and went
into 248, my mother's room.
Her curtain was pulled around her,
as though she was being washed
or changed. My mom was under
a white sheet, her eyes closed,
her mouth open like she was

still struggling to breathe.
Her nurse Julie had tears in her eyes,
wetting her powder blue mask.
The oxygen machine was unplugged,
the blankets rolled up, the neck pillow gone.
I kissed my mom's cold forehead
and hollow cheek. Michele and Kerri did
the same. We whispered as though my mom
could still hear. We were quiet
as three little mice.

Orchid

My sister bought my mother an orchid
to put on her windowsill, something pretty
for her to look at. The orchid needed
to be fed an ice cube three times a week.
When my mother was better, she would
get a piece of ice from her drink and lovingly
place it in the orchid pot herself. Then, for a while
the nurses or my sister and I took over.
The morning my mother died, the orchid
drooped and bowed its browning head.
Maybe it died in sympathy with my mother—
or maybe it was the first time in a while
I thought to look. We were all so busy
at the end, hovering around my mother
fussing to get her to take ice chips.

I Put All the Poems about My Mother's Death in a File

and that night I dream I have my period.
I'm soaking through the pad, rummaging
for clean Kotex under the bathroom cabinet. The pad
is heavy with blood, so cold, so real, so like I remember
life before. I wake up, 61, my sheets dry and clean.
Maybe I have come full circle, the way menstruation
comes full circle, an end, an egg released.
Or had I filled the pad—my notebook?—and
it was time to start a new cycle, put the final period
on my project? My mother and sister and I
sometimes bled together, our bodies in sync.
As a child I was prone to nosebleeds—my first
awareness that blood might come at any time.
The nosebleeds stopped during adolescence,
when I began to bleed below. Shortly after
my father died, my mother took a weekend trip
with her friend. She returned home to find her fridge
on the fritz. She felt so alone. Everything
in the freezer had melted and juice
from the frozen strawberries leaked
through the upper door. My mother called me
sobbing. She said her Maytag was bleeding.

Pink Lady

I stopped eating apples
during the pandemic
when I became afraid
of anyone else touching food
I'd soon consume, before
science understood COVID
didn't live on surfaces.
These were the days
I scoured my doorknobs
with overpriced Clorox wipes,
waiting for news from
the nursing home—would
my mother survive or not?
Apples never came back
into my diet, even when
they were once again
deemed safe. I don't crave
them anymore or miss
that Pink Lady's spray of mist
as I took a knife to slice
it open. I don't miss the crunch
of the peel or the sugary flesh.
Whenever I came across a bruise,
I'd spoon it out—apple bruises
reminding me of my mother's
human ones. How we acclimate,
learn to live without.

A Taste For Bananas

Before she went into the nursing home,
my mother bought three bananas
each week—one yellow, one yellow-ish,
and one green. She sliced a half each
morning on her Honey Bunches of Oats.
It became a family joke—the care
with which she picked her bananas,
how she didn't want to die
with too many bananas left to rot.
She read *The Monkey Goes Bananas*
to Alex, her youngest great-grandson,
who said he didn't like the taste
of bananas at all. "You're breaking
my heart!" my mom said, clutching
her chest in faux distress.
Now that she's gone, Alex knows
how to read the book himself.
He's developed a taste for bananas.
In fact, he loves bananas now.
He looks up to the clouds
telling his GG her heart should be
better now, that he hopes her heart
is no longer broken.

Display

My mother's scoliosis has her leaning
the same way as the palm trees behind her.
She's still standing on her own
wearing the pink lipstick she gave to me
and that I wear now. A yellow shirt is hard
to pull off if you are pale,
and my mom is pale in this photo,
but she looks beautiful, her silver bangs
in the breeze, a palm like a feather in her hair.
And there I am, too, tiny, in the double lenses
of her sunglasses—my torso, my white shirt,
my arms lifting my camera phone. Beyond
her, the lifeguard hut flaps a green flag,
which tells us the waves are mild today,
but for years my mother has been too wobbly
to navigate sand. Beyond her shoulder
is her walker, which I rented at Locatel
Health and Wellness, so she wouldn't have to
lug her own. An employee from Southwest
wheeled her to baggage claim
where I met her. My mother was embarrassed
and gave the woman who pushed her a big tip.
Then I wheeled her to the parking garage,
my mother's suitcase across her lap.
The yellow shirt is my shirt now, but it looks awful
on me. I'll donate it to Goodwill as soon as I can
part with it. My mother once made crazy quilts
and ate kiddy ice cream cups with a wooden spoon.
That is when she could still sit up. That is when
her hands still worked. I transfer this photo
to a thumb drive and take it to CVS.
The man who prints it out says,
What a striking woman. And it strikes me
then—all the mourners will say something
about this photo we display atop the closed casket.

Purse

I emptied her white purse—
tissue pack and reading glasses, coupons
and address book. I once lived in a purse
inside her, my first pink home, the umbilical cord
a knotted strap. When I grew up, I took care
of my own purse, its pristine lining, never stretched
or stuffed with a fetus. I waxed the buckles,
polished the pink clit, the tender button that opened
and closed my clutch. I carried pleasure inside me,
my lips keeping so many secrets.
I tipped my mother's empty purse upside down,
its vulnerable silk insides torn.

After the Tropical Storm

I walk into the Atlantic, the silt so soft
I feel like I'm trudging through mud.
I begin to swim towards the horizon. It is then
I see the baby loggerheads, newly hatched,
the size of quarters, paddling beside me.
When they swerve, I swerve. When they bob
on the surface, so do I. My mother
has just died. I follow the turtles
for two miles at which point I become
one of them, or they one of me, our shells hardening.
We eat kelp and fish eggs, keep each other company.
We grow and have babies of our own.
Theirs are inside eggs. Mine are inside little poems.

Impossible Poem

Sophie Calle, with her mom's permission,
set up a camera to film her last breath,
not knowing, of course, when
it would come. I can't bring myself
to provide any further details
as to what my mother looked like
the morning of her death. The nurses
had cleaned her up, but I can't write more.
Surely you have your own experience
to draw upon—or one day will. We buried
my mother in the ground and divvied up
her belongings—a bureau for my sister,
hutches and tables for my nieces, a chair
for me. Sophie took her mother's portrait,
Chanel necklace, and a diamond ring
to the North Pole, where her mother had always
wanted to go. She buried them all
under a stone on Starvation Glacier.
I took my mother's prayer card and a votive
candle and gathered shells to make an altar
in the sand. My mother loved the waves—
she had been everywhere she ever wanted to go.
I keep trying to craft the right sentence to explain
my mother's impact. Sophie Calle
edited the footage to 11 minutes and called
her film *Impossible to Catch Death*.

Bag Ladies

We returned to get my mother's belongings. It was still the time of COVID,
the summer of Omicron. The orderlies had packed her things for us.
Her clothes were stuffed into bags from the Christmas Tree Shop—
my mother's bags, I guess, from days when she still was out
and about. Colorful plastic totes with handles. My sister and I
just wanted to get out of there, the nursing home lobby with so much sadness
and the daffy receptionist who always asked me if I was "on vacation
in Rhode Island" when I had told her, day after day,
that my mother was in hospice on the second floor.
"Oh that's right," she'd say, looking at my Florida driver's license,
my face that didn't quite match the picture. I was paler, I suppose,
and not smiling. Then she made me sanitize my hands and put on
one of their masks—we weren't allowed to wear our own. We wouldn't
have been allowed to visit my mother those days at all, except
that she was already in hospice, i.e. dying, so getting COVID
wouldn't have mattered to her much. My mother was probably
not even going to be alive long enough for Omicron's
incubation period, though she did live longer than anyone thought.

We returned to pick up the Christmas Tree Shop bags of her clothes.
They kept her shoes and flavored water. They kept her tea towel
with her six great grandsons' faces on it—a gift from one of my nieces
from an online shop where you could put beloveds' pics on anything—
a mug, a sweatshirt, an apron. My sister was upset—didn't want
her smiling grandchildren on another resident's bureau.
But we knew the workers did their best. We didn't want to argue
as long as we had her rosary for the casket. We wanted out
and didn't voice our own fears. I was afraid to die a bag lady,
as 66 percent of single woman are—or so I read in an article. My sister
and I were the matriarchy now, the elders the young ones would
look up to for advice. Were we up to the challenge? My sister and I
didn't voice our fears. Would one of us end up on the street?
Would one of us end up here? Our whole lives stuffed
into two discount store shopping bags on a bright July day?

What We Learned after She Died

My mother used a page torn from *People*—
a picture of Idris Elba (Sexiest Man Alive)—
as a bookmark. When a neighbor boy died
at only 17, my mother was working
in the ER. She drove his little sister
(my friend) back to our house to play
so she wouldn't have to see her parents'
grief. My mother went to her prom
with Al, her best friend's brother, a gay man
who now lives in San Francisco.
She helped my cool older cousin
through a rough patch in her marriage.
I felt I was more her daughter than her niece—
we both always spoke our minds.
Someone named Paula knew her.
Another person named Laraine.
Both women sent cards. Gloria says
She was inscrutable. I never knew
what she was thinking. Ellen says
She sure was sarcastic. But such a good nurse!
My mother donated to causes—
Doctors without Borders, Wounded
Warriors, and MADD since my sister was hit
by a drunk driver her senior year. She donated
even after I'd researched each charity
and told her their dismal ratings.
My sister and I remember playing
with the neighborhood girl—jump
rope, it was summer—remember my mother
saying *Only talk about her brother if she brings it up first.*

Inheritance

My sister gives her grandsons
the Cracker Barrel gift card
my mother never got to use.
They buy candy—Smarties,
Cow Tales, Now and Later:
Long Lasting Chews—
then blow kisses up to their GG,
who now lives beyond the cluttered
ceiling in a gloriously retro heaven
that smells like a Yankee seaside
candle or, maybe, pancakes.

Death Dream

In the dream I keep losing my mother—
the nursing home hallways are crowded,
and when I look at the wheelchair I'm pushing,
it's empty. I turn around and press through,
afraid she's slipped out. I go to a main desk
where an orderly tells me he thinks
he saw her in Room 104, so I hurry there
to find my mother, young again,
sitting upright, biting into a pear.
When I wake, I go to my dream dictionary—
eating the pear indicates success.
But nothing about the significance of 104.
A quick Google search brings me
to an "Angel Number" site, which tells me
Your angel is close to you now,
looking for ways that she can assist.

The Brat

Of course my mother was once a baby
who suckled at my grandmother's breast
and my grandmother was also a baby
and so on. Pre-me, my mother
had a whole life. She was last born,
a menopause baby, a mistake,
though my grandmother was only 36.
The family called her the brat.
My mother was afraid of redheads—
something bad happened to her
when she was little. My guess—a predator
with auburn hair. My mother was a smartie,
an A student, a good girl. Her father
drank a lot and died young, just as
she was off to nursing school.
To prove she wasn't a mistake after all,
she moved back home, became
my Grammy's savior, helped with rent
as her brother and sisters were already
married and out of the house.
My mother was beautiful in her nursing cap,
her cheeks especially pink
in her graduation photo. She always thought
she was fat, even though my father
looked at her with adoring eyes.
She was so tiny when she died—
we called her a model. What a shame
to finally be thin when she couldn't
enjoy it, no way to experiment
with fashion in the nursing home.
A CNA buttoned her up each morning,
half of her clothes lost in the wash,
often wearing another resident's nightgown.
Before my mother's body gave out,
she took care of her mother, my Grammy,

taking her shopping, giving her enemas.
More than once my mother talked her mother
out of suicide. Before my mother's body gave out,
she took care of my father, my sister, and me,
and all those patients in the hospital. When
she was little she was called the brat—
and she spent her life proving
she was anything but.

Mostly Gone

When my father died, his watch stopped.
When my mom died, her digital clock kept telling time.
I took it home with me thinking it would help
wean me off of my phone, which I'd been checking
when I woke up in the middle of the night.
Joan, my mom's hospice roommate,
told me my mom would wake up around 3:00 a.m.
and joke with the nurses. Joan wanted
my sister and me to know our mother,
even at the end, was sometimes "with it."
By the time we visited her in the morning,
my mom was mostly gone. Having Mom's clock
helps. I read the red numbers against the night.
It's 3:35—three more hours to go until breakfast.
All my watches have died, but here I am,
still alive, writing a poem in the dark.
All the watch repair shops I once knew
have closed. Same with cobblers. I keep
the watch my mother bought me years ago,
the one with the pink rhinestone band.
I sometimes wear it as a bracelet,
wishing I could hold my mom's hand.

Circulation

My hands are the coldest
part of me, even in summer.
It's poor circulation or anemia,
the doctor once thought,
and now that I'm older
a pinched nerve in my neck
sends tingles down my arms
making my fingers even icier.
Cold hands, warm heart—
it's true. Life, I am in love
with you. My mother had
the same cold hands, often
warming them by holding
a mug of ginger peach tea.
When she left us, I kissed
her forehead, cold as our hands
which had been preparing us
for this moment. I also have
cold feet, meaning I am
apprehensive about all of this,
though, with death, I know
there's no way to back out.

My Mother's Cover-Up

I bought one for her at Walgreens—teal blue with sparkles. She was so hunched over and short by then, it flowed almost to her ankles. I kept it here in Florida so that when she visited it was one less thing she needed to pack. It was in a drawer along with her one-piece, skirted bathing suit which had adjustable shoulder straps to accommodate her lopsidedness, her scoliosis.

Now that she's gone, I wear the cover-up and mourn each loose sequin, trying to catch the shiny discs as they fall. Walgreens doesn't sell this kind of kaftan anymore—if they did, I would buy more as a way to keep my mother with me.

I walk the seasonal aisle as though it's a metaphor for life itself. Plastic pails and shovels to make dreamy castles, water shoes to protect our feet from rocks, neon noodles to help keep us afloat.

January 6, 2022

A year later, I remember my mom in the nursing home
without her phone. My niece had taken her new clamshell with 4G
to reboot overnight. We hoped this meant her calls
would no longer drop. Kate was sure to save
all my mom's contacts. I'd bought my mom a yearlong plan
of unlimited TracFone minutes, even though she'd only live
seven more months. There was no way to know
that my mother's time would be cut that short. She had survived
COVID—so many in her nursing home gone, buried
because of it. So many, in fact, that they are now raising money
for a Remembrance Garden on the grounds. Of course, COVID
isn't over. And the insurrection continues. A year ago
it seemed unthinkable—camouflage and Confederate flags,
a guillotine, smashed windows, and grown men pooping
on the Capitol floor. Kate dropped off my mother's new phone
at reception as there were still no visitors allowed.
By the time I spoke to my mother she had calmed down
but said the whole nursing home was upset, the Alzheimer's
patients crying and nurses texting their kids. *What if those guys
were able to climb up to the fourth floor?* My mother's legs
wobbled, even with a walker. *I know, Mom,* I said, *I know.*
She asked, *What if I had no way to call you to say goodbye?*
I should have dialed the nurse's station January 6. Should have
insisted I needed to speak to my mother no matter how busy
the staff was. We used to joke about my mother's
burner—the only phone she could dial with her arthritis—
how she was untraceable like the villains in *The Wire*
or *Breaking Bad.* Today I wonder about the contacts
on each rotten Senator's phone. Each rotten Representative
in on the lie. I wonder what they tell their mothers
a year later. That is, if their mothers are still alive.

#MeToo

Before #MeToo, we go to see Louis CK
in Miami. We take a Lyft (my mom's first)
to the Arsht Center, putting her walker in the trunk.
It's November 2016, a little more than a week
after the election. The driver's puzzled—*I can't believe*
you're taking this sweet lady to his show. You know Louis CK
is filthy, right? He looks at me like I'm endangering
my mother who says *Don't let this gray hair*
fool you. I was an ER nurse and probably know
more swear words than you do. The driver gives us
bottles of water and lets us pick the radio station.

A year later, allegations in the *New York Times*
and Louis CK's admission. My mother and I
are befuddled, sure until then he was a feminist.
We loved *Louie* and *Horace and Pete*. (What do Edie Falco
and Jessica Lange and Laurie Metcalf think?)
In November 2017 my apartment is still a mess,
missing walls that were soaked in Hurricane Irma,
then torn down. My mom's in too much pain to make
another trip. We talk on the phone about
Harvey Weinstein, harken back to Bill O'Reilly
and the loofah, Bill Cosby and the Quaaludes.

My mother tells me about handsy doctors
and I tell her about handsy poetry professors.
Neither of us are on Facebook. We barely know
what a hashtag is that fall. And we are
only starting to read about Tarana Burke.
Me too, we keep saying, finally having the language.

Testimony

After he tried to kiss me during office hours,
I ducked and scrambled into the hall
wondering if I had imagined it. After he tried to kiss me,
he dismissed my poems in workshop
though I wondered if I was imagining that too. To move up
the TA waiting list, you were supposed to give the Chair
a blowjob. I wish I were misremembering this. The two women
who received teaching positions thought I was uptight
because I was Catholic. I was drinking
back then—I confess—but no amount of wine
makes this testimony less true. It was the first time
I lived somewhere warm, even in the fall. I wondered
if I would have been safer in mittens and a coat. I wonder
what those two TAs remember of that time, if they feel shame
or rage or have somehow internalized it all.
I never spoke up. I had no words to do so—not even
in my poems, which became conceptual and abstract.
Not even when I dropped out and moved back home
and my mother kept asking me what was wrong.

Signs and No Signs

On my sister's drive home
from Mount St. Rita's, an old man
on a Rascal motions to her
at a stop light. *You're in
the wrong lane!* he says.
My sister still has tears
in her eyes, the sting of
our mother's death,
the panic of all that needs
to be done next. *You're in
the wrong lane!* the man
yells again. *The beauty
pageant contestants are in
the lane over there!*

Poem in Which I Banish Sorrow

I am alive, walking, sun freckling my nose,
no worry yet about my annual mole check.
I have my mother in my pocket—her face
on the prayer card we had printed for her wake.
I ate oatmeal with maple syrup for breakfast
so how can the front page news hurt me?
I lift my zippered wrist pouch where I keep
my keys safe. I strike a Wonder Woman
pose, using my Bracelets of Submission
to deflect the terror of the world.
I know it's a long fight—this untangling
from abuses of power. I am collecting information
about at-home abortions. I am writing down
everything I know about joy as a guide
for future generations—apples, banana bikes,
cubbyholes, Dunkin Donuts, elderberry...

Old Lady Smell

My mother made me promise
to tell her if she ever started to smell
like an old lady. My fastidious mother—
who dusted every Saturday
who never left a dish in the sink overnight
who loved taking showers
(no matter how dangerous they'd become)
who always lifted the lid of her Tupperware
and sniffed her leftovers before eating
who always ran the kitchen fan when she cooked
who always ran the bathroom fan when she pooped
who put a chicken carcass in the freezer
until the day of trash pickup since she didn't want
even her garbage bin to reek—made me pinky swear.
I kept waiting for a human, sour stink
in her house, in the nursing home,
in the hospital, in hospice, on her body
but such a smell never came.
It was as though my mother was a saint,
like Little Rose of Woonsocket—
who died a few months before my mother was born
who performed miracles
who wore the stigmata
who cured the ailments of others
who had crippling arthritis like my mother
who, unlike my mother, died young
whose followers had her grave dug up
to see if she could be canonized by the Catholic Church
whose body hadn't decomposed
whose coffin emanated the scent of roses.

I Have Slept in Many Places

First in the womb, my own space capsule
in my mother's universe, my eyelids sticky with pre-birth,
then the incubator and crib, which I didn't recognize
as a prison until years later when my sister stood inside it
and I, rising from my first big-girl bed, unlatched her
because she was hungry for breakfast. Then my Grammy's
four-poster, kiddy sleeping bag, the hospital bed,
where I was hoarse after I had my tonsils removed. A mat
during kindergarten naptime, the backseat of my mother's car,
another hospital bed with silver bars on the side
where I wrote my first stories. The double bed I shared
with my sister when our twins gave out. A college dorm
mattress with another girl's period stain, a damp study-abroad
bed in Wales, Eurail seats where I could sleep overnight
and save money on a hostel if I picked the right schedule.
Hostel bunk beds with bathrooms down the hall. A friend's
waterbed, another friend's bed on her father's boat.
Then my cousin's hand-me-down mattress
in my first apartment in Boston, a boyfriend's bed
in Revere, a bed of another boy hoping to make
my Revere boyfriend jealous. Sublet beds,
a bed in a furnished studio apartment in Tucson
where there was no way of knowing who'd slept on it
before me. Futon in the East Village right on the floor.
Same futon on a used loft bed to suspend me above the mice.
Then a lavender pullout Mary Richards couch.
Vacation beds, hotel beds. More boyfriend beds
in Brooklyn and Alphabet City. Motel beds.
Florida marital bed and another hospital bed—
this time surgery. Divorce bed (same as marital bed
with mattress flipped for good luck). Evacuation beds
during hurricanes. My true-love's bed with its magic
mattress topper. I know I am forgetting so many places—
subways, lounge chairs in the sand, Amtrak seats,
movie theaters, hammocks, stadium bleachers

at my niece's college graduation (I had taken a Vicodin),
conference beds, beds at university housing
or hotels after I'd given poetry readings, emergency row
plane seats, on my mother's breast when I was an
infant, in my father's arms after a childhood asthma attack.
My parents' bed after their deaths. I'm heading
for the hard coffin bed myself, my eyes sewn shut
against insomnia. I'll stipulate that the undertaker
press glow-in-the-dark stars inside the lid.

Bombs, the Good Kind

My mother's "bomb bars" tasted like Twix. I cut them
into four pieces to make each dose large enough
so she could sleep but not so big that she would get high
and dizzy and trip. She still had her medical marijuana card
though, after she went to the nursing home, cannabis wasn't allowed.
I snuck in cut-up bombs in an Ice Breaker mint case
she could open herself even with her arthritis. She could pop
one after the CNA put her into bed. Then came COVID, so
of course she ran out when I could no longer visit. Gone too
were the vodka nips with the easy-off caps my niece Kate hid
in her top drawer. Oh, the pain was awful and even
my mother's morphine drip didn't always do the trick.
Now whenever I take my own gummy to lessen the pain
in my neck so I can sleep, I think of my mother's painful end.
Will what I have come to rely on be taken away—
like everyone's freedom, one right at a time—tenure and books,
abortions and voting booths? At least we have THC
at the moment to get us through this regressive mess.
When my mother had me, she had no choice. John's mother
told him she tried to throw herself down the stairs—
that's how much she didn't want a kid. I was lucky—
Roe v. Wade during my childbearing years, condoms
during the AIDS crisis, and birth control pills. And now
legal marijuana—bombs, the good kind—raging through
my system. I have friends I hope will bring me a gummy or two
when the time comes, that I won't be alone in a nursing home,
that visitors will be allowed, that I'll suck on a few more
indica chocolate squares to help me sleep.

ACKNOWLEDGMENTS

Grateful acknowledgement to the editors and staff of the following magazines and anthologies where these poems, sometimes in slightly different forms or with slightly different titles, first appeared:

Action, Spectacle: "New Rules"; *American Literary Review*: "Impossible Poem"; *American Poetry Review*: "Mercy" and "Signs and No Signs"; *Axon: Creative Explorations (Australia)*: "I Put All the Poems about My Mother's Death in a File" and "Circulation"; *Bellevue Literary Review*: "Teaspoons"; *Cherry Tree: A National Literary Journal At Washington College*: "The Universe"; *Columbia Poetry Review*: "Prodigal Prayer"; *The Common*: "Strength Training"; *Elm Leaves Journal*: "My Mother in a Grass Skirt," "Pink Lady," "Bag Ladies," and "Bombs, the Good Kind"; *Gargoyle*: "Snow Globe," "Adaptation," "Flip," and "Orchid"; *Glimpse*: "A Taste for Bananas"; *Hanging Loose*: "That's Where You'll Find Me"; *Hole in the Wall*: "Votive Poem"; *Limp Wrist*: "Poem in Which I Banish Sorrow"; *Louisville Review*: "Wackadoodle"; *Marsh Hawk Review*: "ER" and "The Brat"; *Michigan Quarterly Review*: "What My Mother Said in the ICU," "Generosity," and "Inheritance"; *Mollyhouse*: "Barn Babies"; *New England Review*: "Purple Poem"; *North American Review*: "Now That My Mother Isn't Allowed to Walk in the Halls"; *On the Seawall*: "Nourish," "January 6, 2022," and "Old Lady Smell"; *Pine Hills Review*: "What My Mother Left Behind, What She Discarded"; *Plume*: "Butterfly Poem," "The Last Time I Saw My Mother before the Pandemic," "Beginning," "Ready," and "# Me Too"; *Poetry Magazine*: "I Have Slept in Many Places"; *Rattle*: "Monkey Mind (or, Could He Win Again?)" and "Another Summer of Love (2021)"; *Scoundrel Time*: "Laundry Poem," "News," and "My Mother's Cover-Up"; *South Florida Poetry Journal (Soflopojo)*: "Last Picnic" and "Summer of Love"; *Southern Review*: "Display," "Death Dream," and "Mostly Gone"; *SWWIM*: "While She Can Still Speak"; *Thrush Poetry Journal*: "Sweet Day"; *Upstreet*: "Ensure," "Sacrament," "Baby Mouse," "What We Learned after She Died," and "Testimony"; *Westerly (Australia)*: "After the Tropical Storm."

"Independence Day (Hospice)," with artwork by Marlon Portales, and "Another Summer of Love (2021)," with artwork by Natalie Larrodé, are displayed as NFTs on *theVERSEverse*.

"Purse" was published in *From the Belly: Poets Respond to Gertrude Stein's Tender Buttons, Volume I* (edited by Karren Alenier, Word Works Press, 2023).

"Votive Poem" was reprinted in *Dreaming Awake: New Contemporary Prose Poetry from the United States, Australia and England* (edited by Peter Johnson and Cassandra Atherton, Mad Hat Press, 2023).

"Barn Babies," "Strength Training," and "Communique: Emails from Mount St. Rita's" were included in *Four Quartets: Poetry in the Pandemic* (edited by Jeffrey Levine and Kristina Marie Darling, Tupelo Press, 2020).

"Testimony" was reprinted in *Grabbed: Poets & Writers on Sexual Assault, Empowerment & Healing* (edited by Richard Blanco, Caridad Moro, Nikki Moustaki, and Elisa Albo, Beacon Press, 2020).

"Display," "After the Tropical Storm," and "My Mother's Cover-Up" were reprinted in *Southern Voices: The Power of Place* (edited by Andrew Geyer and Tom Mack, Lamar University Literary Press, 2024).

"Death Dream" was reprinted on *Verse Daily*.

"I Have Slept in Many Places" borrows its title from Diane Seuss's [I have slept in many places] published in *frank: sonnets* (Graywolf Press, 2021).

With many thanks to Maureen Seaton, Greg Shapiro, Stephanie Strickland, David Trinidad, and Julie Marie Wade for their input on these poems and their sequencing. And with gratitude to Terrance Hayes, Nancy Krygowski, Jeffrey McDaniel, and Alex Wolfe for their feedback and great care with *Pink Lady*.